TAILGATING

UPPING YOUR GAME

ISBN-13: 978-1-56383-599-5
Item #7147

**Printed in the USA
by G&R Publishing Co.**

Distributed By:

507 Industrial Street
Waverly, IA 50677

www.cqbookstore.com

gifts@cqbookstore.com

 CQ Products

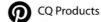 CQ Products

 @cqproducts

 @cqproducts

Inside, we're giving you THE yummiest recipes to help you pull off a simply fantastic tailgating menu. Below, we share our favorite tips to get you down the road to pre-game success.

TIPS BEFORE THE TIP-OFF

1 Prepare as much of the food as possible in advance. Premix the drinks, marinate the chicken, patty the burgers, make the dips, and pack the brownies.

2 If you're headed to the game, check the venue's website for tailgating rules so there are no surprises when you arrive.

3 Consider packing one cooler for food and a separate one for drinks.

4 Frozen bottles of water will not only keep food cold in your cooler, but will also give you ice-cold drinking water as the ice melts.

5 If you're grilling, make sure you have more fuel or charcoal than you think you'll need. Also, think about how you'll pack and bring home a dirty grill.

6 Heavy-duty aluminum foil and disposable foil pans are great for reheating food on the grill.

7 Take along trash bags or big plastic bins for hauling out your trash when you leave.

8 Pack a few portable chairs and a table.

9 Using a tablecloth makes for easier cleanup, no matter where you are.

10 Disposable wet wipes or good ol' soap and water are a must for messy fingers. Wiping hands on game-day jerseys is not recommended.

HAPPINESS IS...TAILGATING WITH FRIENDS!

SHOW-YOUR-COLORS *Fruit Salad*

- 2 C. chopped fresh strawberries
- 2 (15 oz.) cans mandarin oranges, drained
- 2 C. chopped fresh apricots or peaches
- 2 C. green grapes
- 2 C. red grapes
- ¼ C. honey
- Zest and juice of 1 lime
- 2 C. fresh blackberries or blueberries

In a big bowl, combine the strawberries, mandarin oranges, apricots, and all the grapes. In a small bowl, whisk together the honey, lime zest, and lime juice. Chill until serving time.

When you're ready to eat, add the blackberries and the honey mixture to the big bowl of fruit; stir gently until coated. **Makes about 12 cups**

STORAGE IDEA

Pack salads and other side dishes into square containers with lids. They stack perfectly in your cooler, they're easy to grab at chow time, and if by chance there are any leftovers, just stack them back in your cooler.

4

PEANUT & CRACKER JACK *Bars*

Preheat the oven to 350° and butter a 9 x 13" baking pan; line with parchment paper, letting about 1" hang over two sides. Set aside.

In a mixing bowl, beat together 1 C. melted butter and 1¼ C. brown sugar until smooth. Add 2 eggs, one at a time, beating well after each. Mix in 1 tsp. vanilla and ½ tsp. salt; add 2 C. flour and beat until just incorporated. Gently fold in ½ C. chopped salted peanuts and spread batter evenly in the prepped pan; sprinkle with 3 heaping cups Cracker Jacks and ¼ C. chopped salted peanuts, pressing down gently to adhere. Bake 25 to 30 minutes, until golden brown and firm to the touch. Set aside to cool. Remove from the pan using the parchment paper and cut into squares. **Makes 12**

CROWD-CRUISIN' *Brat Pizzas*

Toss 3 or 4 precooked brats or smoked sausages on the grill until heated through and as charred as you like. Take 'em off the grill and cut into slices. Remove the six rolls from a 10 oz. pkg. of frozen cheese ciabatta rolls *(they can be thawed first or used frozen)* and set cheese side up on a foil-lined grill grate. Grill over low heat until heated through. Remove from the heat and spread with your favorite BBQ sauce. Top with shredded mozzarella cheese, the grilled brat slices, roasted red peppers *(drained and sliced)*, and chopped pickles *(dill or sweet)*. Return them to the grill, close the lid, and heat until the cheese melts. **Makes 6**

DOUBLE-PLAY *Chicken Skewers*

6 boneless, skinless chicken thighs

3 to 4 chipotle peppers in adobo sauce

½ C. orange juice

¼ C. lime juice

2 T. canola oil

1 tsp. garlic salt

1 to 2 T. hot chili powder

1 tsp. whole black peppercorns

Salt to taste

2 or 3 limes, optional

If you'll be using wooden skewers, soak them in water overnight.

Depending on the size and shape of the chicken thighs, push two or three skewers through each thigh, leaving at least 1" between skewers. Set them in a single layer in a big rimmed pan.

Finely chop the chipotle peppers and toss them into a bowl. Whisk in the orange and lime juices, oil, garlic salt, chili powder, and peppercorns. Pour the mixture over the chicken, cover, and refrigerate 1 to 4 hours.

Line the grill grate with foil and spritz with cooking spray; preheat the grill to medium-high. Remove the chicken from the marinade and sprinkle with salt. Grill until golden brown on both sides and cooked through (165°), turning once. Remove from the grill and let rest 5 minutes. In the meantime, cut the limes in half and grill until marked if you'd like; squeeze their juice over the chicken. Cut each thigh between the skewers, creating individual pieces and making them super easy to grab and eat. Remove the peppercorns before eating.
Serves 6

TWISTED 'RITAS

In a 1-qt. mason jar, combine 1 C. fresh lime juice, 1 C. silver tequila, 1 C. 7-Up, and 2 T. lime simple syrup; add 1 sliced lime and fill with ice. Cover, shake, and strain into ice-filled glasses.* **Makes about 4 C.**

*For lime simple syrup, dissolve 1 C. sugar in ½ C. each water and fresh lime juice in a small saucepan; cool before using. Keep extra in the fridge for up to 2 weeks.

9

FARM TEAM *Deviled Eggs*

6 eggs

2 T. mayo

1½ T. sweet pickle relish

1 tsp. prepared yellow
  mustard

⅛ tsp. salt

Dash of black pepper

Paprika

Put the eggs in a single layer in a saucepan and add water to cover by 1". Bring to a boil; cover, remove from the heat, and let stand 15 minutes.

Drain the water off the eggs, then fill the saucepan with cold water and ice; let stand until the eggs are cool.

Peel the eggs under cold running water and slice them in half lengthwise. Using a spoon, remove the yolks and toss them into a bowl along with the mayo, relish, mustard, salt, and black pepper; mash and stir until well combined. Spoon the yolk mixture into hollowed-out egg whites and sprinkle with paprika. **Makes 1 dozen**

Bacon BARNSTORMERS

Cook eggs as indicated above. Mash the yolks and stir in 3 cooked and crumbled bacon strips, 3 T. ranch dressing, and a dash of black pepper; spoon into hollowed-out egg whites. Top with additional bacon or jalapeño slices for extra kick.

MAIN EVENT *Beer Burgers*

1½ lbs. extra lean ground beef

3 T. finely chopped onion

1 tsp. minced garlic

2 T. Worcestershire sauce

⅓ C. of your favorite beer *(we used chocolate porter)*

1½ tsp. olive oil

1½ tsp. salt

Black pepper

Butter, softened

6 hamburger buns, split *(we used onion buns)*

Mayo

Tomato slices

Combine ground beef, onion, garlic, Worcestershire sauce, beer, oil, salt, and ½ teaspoon black pepper and mix gently with your hands. Form six equal patties, press an indentation in the middle of each, and chill for at least an hour.

Grease the cooking grate of a grill and preheat the grill on medium-high heat. Grill the burgers to desired doneness. During the last minute or two of grilling, butter the cut sides of the buns and set them butter side down to toast. Put a pat of butter on each burger as you take it off the grill.

Put a burger and tomato slice on a toasted bun bottom and add a dash of pepper. Slather mayo on the top toasted bun as the finishing touch to this truly delicious burger. **Makes 6**

COOL IDEA

Freeze water in plastic milk jugs to use as jumbo ice blocks in your cooler.

TOURNAMENT *Tortilla Twirls*

- 6 oz. cream cheese, softened
- 12 oz. sour cream
- 2 T. taco seasoning
- ½ (16 oz.) can refried beans *(we used black bean refried beans)*
- 8 (10") flour tortillas
- 1 C. frozen peas, thawed

- ½ C. shredded carrot
- ½ C. thinly sliced green onions *(white and light green parts)*
- 1 (11 oz.) can Mexi-corn, well drained
- 1½ C. finely shredded Mexican cheese blend

Combine cream cheese and sour cream in a mixing bowl and beat until smooth. Mix in taco seasoning until well combined.

Spread some of the refried beans down the middle of each tortilla. Spread the cream cheese mixture on both sides of the beans, leaving about ½" uncovered around the edge of the tortillas. Sprinkle evenly with peas, carrot, green onions, corn, and cheese. Fold in the sides of the tortillas and roll up tightly. Wrap in plastic wrap and chill overnight.

Unwrap the tortillas and use a sharp knife to cut each into 1" slices before serving.
Serves a crowd

SIDELINE SLAMMERS

In a 2-qt. pitcher or lidded jar, mix 2 (16.9 oz.) bottles Dr. Pepper, ¾ C. apple-flavored whisky, and ¼ C. grenadine. Serve over ice.
Makes about 5¼ C.

To make these football-inspired drink glasses, cut white vinyl or label stickers to desired size and attach to dry glasses.

Smoky HALFTIME *Hummus*

Drain 1 (15 oz.) can chickpeas, reserving the liquid. Rinse the chickpeas under cold water and dump into a food processor. Add 2 roasted red bell peppers, ½ C. sun-dried tomato halves, ¼ C. tahini, 1 chopped garlic clove, and 3 T. olive oil; pulse until relatively smooth. With the machine running, slowly add 5 T. of the reserved chickpea liquid; season with salt, black pepper, cayenne pepper, and paprika to taste. Portion out into individual serving bowls for easy eating. Serve with fresh veggies *(try carrots, tomatoes, bell peppers, cucumbers, and zucchini)*. **Makes 1½ cups**

Need a break from heavy tailgating food? Far from boring, this unique hummus is the perfect combination of sweet and smoky.

TAILGATE *Spinach Salad*

Cook 1 C. orzo pasta according to package directions. In the meantime, in a big bowl, whisk together 3 T. olive oil, 3 T. red wine vinegar, 1 tsp. Italian or Mediterranean seasoning blend, and salt and black pepper to taste.

Drain the pasta and rinse with cold water; add to the bowl and stir to coat. Gently stir in 4 C. lightly packed baby spinach *(coarsely chopped)*, ¼ C. chopped dried tomatoes *(packed in oil)*, and about 12 pitted Kalamata olives *(sliced)*.
Makes about 5 cups

A tangy pasta salad with a distinctive Mediterranean vibe – and no mayo in sight! Perfect for any game-day appetite.

HIGH OCTANE *Chili*

½ onion, diced

1 lb. lean ground beef

1 tsp. vegetable oil

1 (6 oz.) can Italian tomato paste

1 (15 oz.) can chili beans

1 (15 oz.) can black beans, drained & rinsed

1 (14 oz.) can fire-roasted tomatoes with garlic

1 (16 oz.) bottle dark beer *(we used porter)*

1 tsp. sugar

Salt, black pepper, cayenne pepper, and chili powder to taste

Your favorite chili toppings

Cook the onion and beef in hot oil until done, crumbling it while it cooks. Stir in the tomato paste, all the beans, tomatoes, beer, sugar, salt, black pepper, cayenne pepper, and chili powder. Simmer 30 minutes or so, until thick and yummy, or transfer to a slow cooker and let it cook until you're ready to eat.

Load up with your favorite toppings or eat it plain. Either way, it's spectacular! **Makes about 8 cups**

Chili is a great tailgating food – it can be prepped hours or even days ahead of time, then chilled and reheated when needed.

MVP *Snack Mix*

In a big paper grocery bag, combine 1 (7 oz.) box Cheez-It crackers, 1 (8 to 9 oz.) pkg. oyster crackers, 1 (9 oz.) can salted cashews, 1 (7.5 oz.) bag Bugles snacks, and 1 (16 oz.) bag small pretzel twists. In a pint mason jar, combine ¾ to 1 C. canola oil, 2 (1 oz.) pkgs. dry ranch dressing mix, and 2 T. dill weed; screw on the lid and shake until well combined. Drizzle over the cracker combo and roll the bag closed; shake to coat everything. Spread on paper towels to dry at room temperature, or divide among two parchment paper-lined jelly roll pans and bake at 325° for 10 to 15 minutes, then spread on paper towels to cool. Store in airtight containers. **Serves a crowd**

THAI-D GAME *Turkey Wraps*

Dice ¾ lb. grilled and cooled turkey breast and toss into a big bowl. Add 1½ C. coleslaw mix, several thinly sliced and halved radishes, 3 thinly sliced green onions, a handful of chopped fresh cilantro, and a handful of dry-roasted peanuts; toss to combine. In a small bowl, whisk together 3 T. each creamy peanut butter, soy sauce, lime juice, brown sugar, and sesame oil. Whisk in 1½ tsp. minced garlic, a pinch of red pepper flakes, and salt and black pepper to taste. Pour the sauce over the cabbage mixture and toss to coat thoroughly. Put a few lettuce leaves on 4 (10") flour tortillas, then divide the chicken mixture evenly over the lettuce. Fold in the sides of the tortillas and roll up. Cut in half to serve. **Makes 4 full-size wraps**

VICTORY-IS-OURS *Margarita Bars*

1 C. butter, softened

1 C. coarsely crushed pretzels

3½ C. sugar, divided

Flour

3 limes

½ C. tequila or lime juice

6 large eggs at room temperature

½ C. powdered sugar

Preheat the oven to 350°. Mix the butter, pretzels, ½ cup of the sugar, and 1 cup plus 1 tablespoon flour until well combined. Spread evenly in the bottom and ¼" to ½" up the sides of a greased 9 x 13" baking pan. Bake 12 to 15 minutes or until light golden brown. Remove from the oven and set aside while you make the filling. Don't turn off the oven.

Zest the limes and then squeeze their juice into a 1-cup measuring cup until you have about ½ cup of juice; fill to the 1 cup mark with tequila and pour the mixture into a big bowl. Stir in the eggs, the remaining 3 cups sugar, 1 cup flour, and about ⅔ of the zest until well combined; pour the filling into the partially cooled crust. Bake for an additional 30 to 35 minutes or until the center is set. Set aside until cool. Meanwhile mix the remaining lime zest with the powdered sugar; set aside.

When the bars are cool, cut into serving-size pieces. Stir the powdered sugar mixture and sprinkle evenly over the bars.
Makes 18

PIGSKIN PRETZELS

Cook ½ lb. maple-flavored bacon until crisp; drain, cool, and chop. Melt ½ (24 oz.) pkg. chocolate or vanilla almond bark according to package directions. Coat 8 pretzel rods with the melted bark, leaving about ¼ of the length of each uncoated; set on waxed paper. While the chocolate is still wet, sprinkle with half the bacon; repeat with 8 more pretzels.
Makes 16

23

PIGPILE *Pork Burgers*

2 lbs. ground pork
1 tsp. ground ginger
½ C. diced green onion
¼ tsp. ground allspice
Salt and black pepper
  to taste
BBQ sauce

6 pineapple rings
Butter
6 hamburger buns
Spinach leaves
6 slices deli ham

Dump ground pork, ginger, green onion, allspice, salt, and black pepper into a bowl and mix with your hands until just combined. Form six large patties and press an indentation in the middle of each.

Grease the grill grates and preheat the grill on medium heat. Toss the patties on the grill and brush with BBQ sauce; cook with the lid closed until brown on the bottom, then flip and brush with more sauce. Cook until done *(160°)*, then set aside for 5 minutes. In the meantime, toss the pineapple slices on the grate and heat until lightly browned, turning once. Butter the cut sides of the buns and set them butter side down until nicely toasted.

Build your burgers with spinach, more BBQ sauce, a slice of ham, and a grilled pineapple slice, all sandwiched between the grilled buns. Enjoy! **Makes 6**

Extra points given for not burning the buns!

JUST CHILLIN' *Pasta Salad*

Cook 1 lb. pasta *(we used shells, but any small shape will work)* to al dente, according to package directions; drain, rinse with cold water, and set aside to cool. Meanwhile, chop up ½ red onion, 1 green bell pepper, and 3 celery ribs and toss them into a big bowl. Cut 4 oz. cheddar cheese into small cubes and add to the bowl along with ½ to 1 (5 oz.) pkg. mini pepperoni. In a small bowl, whisk together ½ C. creamy Italian dressing, 2 T. mayo, and enough dried basil, salt, and black pepper to make your taste buds happy; add to the cooled pasta and stir to blend. Serve immediately or chill first *(if chilled, add a little more Italian dressing at serving time if it seems dry)*. **Serves a crowd**

RAH-RAH *Chex Mix*

Line a big work surface with waxed paper. In a big saucepan over medium heat *(or in a really big microwave-safe bowl on 50% power in the microwave)*, melt together 1 C. butter, 1 (11.5 oz.) bag milk chocolate chips, and 1 (10 oz.) bag dark chocolate chips; remove from the heat and stir in 1 C. malted milk powder. Quickly stir in 2 (12.8 oz.) boxes Chocolate Chex cereal until coated *(you might need to get in there with your hands to break apart the clumps).* Spread out on the waxed paper to cool. Then mix in a 10-oz. bag of mini marshmallows and a 10-oz. pkg. malted milk balls until combined. Eat them as is or dump into a brown grocery bag with 2 C. powdered sugar and shake to coat. Or make everybody happy and shake half the Chex mixture with half the powdered sugar and mix together with the plain batch for half-and-half scrumptiousness. **Serves a crowd**

JUMBOTRON *Stud Muffins*

4 T. unsalted butter
¼ C. vegetable oil
Sugar
1 egg
1 egg white
1½ tsp. vanilla
½ C. buttermilk

1¾ C. flour
2 tsp. baking powder
2 tsp. cornstarch
½ tsp. salt
1 C. semi-sweet chocolate chips

In a glass mixing bowl, melt the butter in the microwave; cool 5 minutes, then stir in the oil. Add 1 cup of sugar, the egg, egg white, and vanilla and stir until well combined. Stir in the buttermilk.

In a separate bowl, mix the flour, baking powder, cornstarch, and salt. Fold the dry ingredients into the wet ingredients until barely combined and then gently stir in the chocolate chips until just combined *(don't overmix)*. Cover the bowl with a towel and let rest 15 minutes. Meanwhile, preheat the oven to 425°.

Line jumbo muffin tins with liners and divide the batter among them. Sprinkle the top of each muffin with about 1 tablespoon sugar and bake for 8 minutes; keep muffins in the oven while you reduce the heat to 350° and bake 15 minutes longer, until tops are just beginning to turn golden. **Makes 6**

WIDE-EYED COLD BREW

The night before, put ½ C. ground coffee in a 1-qt. mason jar; fill with water, cover, and let set overnight at room temp. Strain through a coffee filter; discard solids and pour liquid into a clean mason jar. Fill jar with water. To serve, fill a 1-pt. jar with ice; fill ⅔ full with coffee mixture, add a big splash of half & half, and sweetened condensed milk to taste. Stir, sip, and say, "Good morning!" **Makes 6 to 8 servings**

GRILLED DOGS: BEYOND BASIC

Start by grilling your favorite dogs over medium or medium-high heat – light to dark char, your choice. Score bonus points for grilling the buns. Now, step up your game with mind-blowing toppings for doggie heaven deliciousness! **Servings vary**

CHIP & DIP *Dawgs*

Put the grilled hot dogs in those nicely toasted buns *(you toasted 'em, right?)*. Then add a big mound of French Onion dip, a handful of chopped red onion, and some coarsely crushed potato chips. Be warned – you may have the urge to chase your tail. Yeah, they're THAT good!

MACHO NACHO *Dogs*

Spread refried beans on grilled buns, add grilled hot dogs, shredded longhorn cheese, chopped onion, and pickled or fresh jalapeño slices. Set on foil and return to the grill; close the lid and heat until the cheese melts. Remove from the grill and hit 'em with sour cream and chopped tomato. Howlin' delicious!

JACKED-UP *Pups*

Grill hot dogs on one side and remove from the grill. Flip 'em over and slice lengthwise, without cutting all the way through. Stuff with shredded Colby Jack cheese. Set on foil and finish grilling cheese side up, until the cheese is melty. Put dogs in grilled buns, top with BBQ sauce, yellow mustard, diced avocado, chopped cooked bacon, and more cheese. Yip-Yip-Yippee!

PRE-GAME *Chips & Fruit Salsa*

- 2 T. sugar
- 1 T. brown sugar
- 3 T. fruit preserves, any flavor *(we used raspberry)*
- 2 kiwis, peeled & diced
- 2 Golden Delicious apples, diced
- 1 (6 oz.) pkg. fresh raspberries
- 1 lb. fresh strawberries, diced
- 1 C. fresh blueberries
- 10 (10") flour tortillas
- Cooking spray
- Cinnamon-sugar

In a big bowl, mix the sugar, brown sugar, and preserves until well combined. Add the kiwis, apples, raspberries, strawberries, and blueberries; stir to blend. Cover and chill.

Preheat the oven to 350°. Coat one side of each tortilla with cooking spray. Sprinkle with cinnamon-sugar and spritz again with cooking spray. Cut each tortilla into eight wedges and arrange in a single layer on baking sheets. Bake on the bottom oven rack for 10 to 15 minutes, until lightly browned; cool.

If you're traveling, pack the chips lightly in an airtight container or big zippered plastic bags. *(Don't forget to grab the Fruit Salsa from the fridge, and make sure you pack a serving spoon – unless you're a fan of double-dipping.)*
Serves a crowd

CHAMPION *Breakfast Burritos*

1 lb. bacon, diced

8 frozen hash brown patties

Salt and black pepper to taste

16 eggs

2 T. water

1 T. butter

8 (10") flour tortillas

1 green bell pepper, diced

2 C. shredded sharp cheddar cheese

Salsa and sour cream, optional

Cook the bacon and hash brown patties in separate skillets until crisp; season potatoes with salt and black pepper and drain everything on paper towels. Whisk together the eggs and water until light. Melt the butter in a big skillet over medium-low heat and pour in the eggs. Cook until set but still wet-looking, stirring occasionally.

Set each flour tortilla on a square of foil big enough to wrap around a burrito. Top each tortilla with a cooked hash brown patty. Divide the cooked bacon, bell pepper, cheese, and cooked eggs evenly over the top. Fold two sides of the tortillas over the filling, then roll up burrito-style; wrap tightly with foil.

Set the foil-wrapped burritos on a medium-hot grill, rotating until heated through. Unwrap and top with salsa and sour cream if you'd like. **Makes 8 full-size burritos**

CARIBBEAN HAIL MARYS

*In a 2-qt. pitcher, combine 4½ C. chilled tomato juice (regular for those of you who are timid; spicy for the daring-at-heart), 1½ C. spiced rum, 1½ T. Worcestershire sauce, 1 to 1½ T. hot sauce, 1 to 1½ tsp. each celery salt, coarse salt, and coarse black pepper, and the juice from 1 lemon and 1½ limes. Stir and pour into ice-filled glasses. Garnish as you wish. **Makes about 7 C.***

FANFARE *Queso*

Brown ½ lb. spicy pork sausage, crumbling it while it cooks; drain and dump into a 2-qt. baking dish. Stir in ¾ C. pale ale *(or another fave)*, 16 oz. Velveeta *(cubed)*, ½ C. shredded Pepper Jack cheese, 1 (14.5 oz.) can Mexican seasoned tomatoes *(undrained)*, and 1 C. black beans *(drained & rinsed)*. Bake at 350° for 30 minutes, or until the cheese is melted and everything is nice and hot. Stir in ¼ C. chopped fresh cilantro. Serve with taco-flavored Doritos. **Serves a crowd**

To make in a slow cooker, simply toss the browned and drained pork with the other ingredients into a 2-qt. cooker; heat on high for 2 to 3 hours. Or heat on the grill by putting the ingredients into a 2-qt. disposable foil pan; cover with foil and heat until warm and melty.

WINNING *Sugar Cookies*

Cream 1 C. unsalted butter *(softened)* in a mixing bowl, then gradually beat in ¾ C. sugar. Beat in 1 egg, 2 tsp. vanilla, and ¼ tsp. salt until well mixed. Stir in 2½ C. flour, a little at a time, until incorporated. Divide the dough in half, wrap in plastic, and chill overnight. Remove dough from fridge and let stand at room temperature until softened. Roll out on a floured surface to ¼" thickness and cut out as desired *(baseballs, footballs, race cars ... the choice is yours)*. Bake on cookie sheets lined with parchment paper at 350° for 12 to 15 minutes, until the edges just start to turn brown; remove from the cookie sheets and cool.

Decorate as desired using your favorite frosting. Wait until set before packing into a container, with waxed paper between layers. **Makes about 2 dozen 2½" cookies**

STICK-IT-TO-'EM *Kabobs*

½ C. soy sauce

¼ C. rice wine vinegar

3 T. honey

1 T. toasted sesame oil

4 cloves garlic

2 lbs. flank or sirloin steak, trimmed

3 big bell peppers, any color

1 big red onion

Coarse salt and black pepper

If you'll be using wooden skewers, soak them in water overnight.

Put the soy sauce, vinegar, honey, oil, and garlic in a gallon-size zippered bag; close and squeeze to combine, then remove about ¼ cup and put in a separate container for later. Cut the steak into 1½ to 2" chunks and add them to the bag; chill for 1 to 8 hours.

Preheat a grill on medium-high heat. Cut the bell peppers and onion into 1½ to 2" chunks and slide onto skewers alternately with the marinated steak chunks. Brush some of the marinade from the bag over the food, season with salt and black pepper, and grill until they're done to your liking, turning occasionally.

After removing from the grill, let the skewers rest for 5 minutes, then brush with the marinade you set aside earlier. **Serves 6 to 8**

Nothing smells better than steak on the grill. No need to gather the gang to eat – they'll come running!

39

HOO-YA *Hoagie Dip*

1 medium onion

2 pickled banana peppers

½ head iceberg lettuce

1 big tomato, seeded

1 (3 oz.) pkg. thinly sliced genoa salami

1 (7 oz.) pkg. each thinly sliced honey ham and roasted turkey breast

¼ lb. thinly sliced white cheddar cheese

½ C. mayo

1 T. olive oil

1 tsp. dried oregano

1½ tsp. dried basil

¼ tsp. red pepper flakes

1 (10 to 12") round bread loaf *(we used ciabatta)*

8 hoagie rolls

Chop the onion, peppers, lettuce, tomato, salami, ham, turkey, and cheese and toss into a bowl.

In a separate bowl, whisk together the mayo, oil, oregano, basil, and pepper flakes; add to the meat mixture, stirring until well combined. Chill until ready to serve.

Carve out the center of the round bread loaf, keeping the sides and bottom intact. Pack the meat mixture into the hollowed-out bread. Cut the bread scraps and the hoagie rolls into big chunks.

To serve, mound the dip onto bread chunks and enjoy a mouthful. **Serves 8**

HOO-YA *Hoagies*

Eliminate the round bread loaf — no need for that here. Mix all the ingredients except the lettuce as directed above and simply mound the mixture on lettuce-lined hoagie rolls. Super easy. Just as yummy.

POUND-'EM *Brown Sugar Cake*

½ C. shortening

½ C. sugar

2¾ C. brown sugar, divided

1¼ C. butter, softened, divided

3 tsp. vanilla, divided

5 eggs

3 C. flour

½ tsp. baking powder

¼ tsp. salt

1¼ C. milk, divided

1¼ C. toasted, chopped pecans, divided

2 C. powdered sugar, sifted

Preheat the oven to 350°. Spray a 10" tube pan with cooking spray; set aside. In a mixing bowl, beat the shortening, sugar, 2¼ cups brown sugar, 1 cup butter, and 2 teaspoons vanilla. Add the eggs, one at a time, beating well after each. In a separate bowl, mix the flour, baking powder, and salt; add to the butter mixture alternately with 1 cup of the milk, beating well. Stir in 1 cup of the pecans; spread in the prepped pan. Bake 1¼ hours or until a wooden skewer inserted in the center comes out clean, covering with foil during last 15 minutes to prevent overbrowning. Set on a cooling rack for 10 minutes, then remove the cake from the pan and set upright to cool.

Melt the remaining ¼ cup butter in a saucepan over medium-low heat. Add the remaining ½ cup brown sugar and cook 2 minutes, stirring constantly. Add the remaining ¼ cup milk and bring to a boil, stirring constantly. Remove from the heat and stir in the remaining 1 teaspoon vanilla. Whisk in the powdered sugar until smooth, and immediately spread over the cooled cake; quickly sprinkle with the remaining ¼ cup pecans, pressing to adhere. Slice and serve. **Serves 12 to 15**

OPPOSING TEAM BITES

Put about 65 small pretzel twists on waxed paper-lined rimmed trays. Mix 1 C. creamy peanut butter, 2 T. softened butter, ¾ C. brown sugar, and enough sifted powdered sugar until no longer sticky (½ C. or more). Put about a teaspoon of the mixture on each pretzel and lightly press another pretzel on top. Freeze 30 minutes. Dip each pretzel halfway into melted chocolate almond bark; let dry. **Makes about 65**

SEASON TICKET *Picnic 'Wiches*

½ C. mayo

½ C. sour cream

¼ C. prepared horseradish

¼ to ½ tsp. lemon zest

Coarse salt and
   black pepper

Hot sauce to taste

6 hoagie or steak rolls

3 or 4 tomatoes, sliced

1½ lbs. sliced deli
   roast beef

Lettuce

1 red onion, thinly sliced

Mix the mayo, sour cream, horseradish, lemon zest, and 1¼ teaspoons salt. Season generously with black pepper and hot sauce. Cover and chill at least 30 minutes.

When you're ready to eat, spread the chilled horseradish sauce over the bottom half of the rolls *(or serve it alongside the sandwiches instead)*. Add some tomato slices and season with salt and pepper. Top with roast beef, lettuce, and onion. Cut in half for serving. **Makes 6 full-size sandwiches**

These sandwiches will hold up for several hours. If you're going to make these even further ahead than that, leave off the tomatoes and the horseradish sauce and add those at serving time. Wrap the sandwiches in plastic, foil, or parchment paper and use string to hold in place, making it easier to eat; keep chilled.

TAILGATER'S BEST *Fiesta Cups*

Stir together ½ (16 oz.) can refried beans and ½ to 1 (1.25 oz.) pkg. taco seasoning mix until well blended; divide evenly among six 5-oz. cups. Over the bean mixture in each cup, spread a heaping tablespoon each guacamole, sour cream, and salsa. Sprinkle 1 to 2 T. shredded cheddar cheese over the salsa and top with sliced green onions, sliced black olives, and diced tomatoes; cover and chill until serving time. Serve with tortilla or corn chips. **Makes 6**

Use the remainder of the refried beans to make Macho Nacho Dogs, page 31.

HANDS-OFF *Meatballs*

Preheat the oven to 350°. Combine 2 lbs. extra lean ground beef, 1 C. Italian seasoned bread crumbs, 1 egg, ⅔ C. diced onion, 1 tsp. salt, ½ tsp. black pepper, and 1 tsp. each dried basil, oregano, and parsley. Mix with your hands until blended. Shape into 24 (2") meatballs and arrange on a greased rimmed baking sheet. Bake 20 to 30 minutes, until done *(160°)*. Place the cooked meatballs in a 3-qt. slow cooker. Whisk together 1 (18 oz.) bottle BBQ sauce and 1 (12 oz.) jar grape jelly and pour the mixture over the meatballs. Heat on low for a few hours to combine flavors.
Makes 24

BASES LOADED *Potato Salad*

3 eggs
3 lbs. red-skinned potatoes
Salt
8 dill pickle spears, diced
3 celery ribs, sliced
½ medium red onion,
    chopped

⅔ C. mayo
2 T. stone-ground mustard
2½ T. apple cider vinegar
2 T. chopped fresh dill weed
Black pepper

Put the eggs in a single layer in a saucepan and add water to cover by 1". Bring to a boil; cover, remove from heat, and let stand 15 minutes. Drain, then fill the saucepan with cold water and ice; let stand until the eggs are cool. Peel under cold running water and set aside.

In the meantime, in a big saucepan, cook the potatoes in salted boiling water until just tender; drain and cool. Cut the potatoes into bite-size pieces and dump into a big bowl along with the pickles, celery, and onion.

In a small bowl, stir together the mayo, mustard, vinegar, and dill; pour the mixture over the vegetables in the bowl. Dice the cooled eggs and add to the bowl. Season with salt and black pepper and mix gently until blended. **Serves 8 to 10**

Potato salad is an all-time favorite. Keep it well chilled until serving time, then return it to the cooler within 2 hours (sooner if it's hot outside).

HOMERUN ANTIPASTO

Slide antipasto-type ingredients onto skewers for a great walk-around appetizer. Chill until ready to serve. Try any combination of yummy items, such as cherry peppers, sweet banana peppers, mini bell peppers, pickled vegetables, marinated artichoke hearts, black olives, stuffed green olives, Kalamata olives, cherry tomatoes, small marinated mozzarella balls, cheese cubes, small mushrooms, salami, summer sausage, and prosciutto.
Servings vary

Cheesy Chicken SLIDERS

- 1¼ lbs. boneless, skinless chicken breasts
- 1 (12 oz.) can or bottle plus ½ C. beer *(your favorite)*, divided
- 2 garlic cloves, minced
- 1 tsp. each salt and black pepper
- ¼ tsp. Tabasco sauce
- 1 lb. Velveeta, cubed
- Prepared yellow mustard
- 10 to 12 slider or cocktail buns, split
- 2 T. chopped fresh chives

Put the chicken, 12 oz. beer, garlic, salt, and black pepper in a 1½-quart slow cooker. Cover and cook on low 6 to 8 hours. *(In a hurry? Cook on high 3 to 4 hours instead.)* Shred the chicken thoroughly and stir back into the juices in the cooker.

In the meantime, for the cheese sauce, pour the remaining ½ cup beer into a separate 1-quart slow cooker. Add the Tabasco and Velveeta. Cover and cook on high 45 to 50 minutes, until melted; stir until smooth. *(You can keep the cheese sauce warm and melty on low for up to 4 hours.)*

Spread mustard on the buns and top with chicken, cheese sauce, and chives. **Makes 10 to 12**

PIT CREW *Brownies*

½ C. plus 2 T. butter, softened

6 T. unsweetened cocoa powder

A big handful of semi-sweet chocolate chips

1¼ C. sugar

1½ tsp. vanilla

3 eggs

1¼ C. flour

¼ tsp. salt

½ C. chopped mixed nuts

Preheat the oven to 350°. Grease the bottom only of an 8" square baking pan.

In a saucepan over low heat, melt together ½ cup of the the butter, cocoa powder, and chocolate chips, stirring occasionally. Remove from the heat and stir in the sugar and vanilla. Add eggs one at a time, stirring well after each addition. Stir in the flour and salt until well combined and smooth. Stir in the nuts.

Spread the mixture evenly in the prepped pan and bake 25 to 32 minutes, until the brownies just begin to pull away from the sides of the pan. Do not over-bake. Cool completely before cutting. **Makes 9**

Banana Split STICKS

Cut cooled brownies into bite-size squares. Push onto wooden skewers alternately with banana chunks, pineapple chunks, and strawberries. For extra yum, serve with marshmallow ice cream topping for dipping. **Servings vary**

WALK-AND-TALK *Tacos*

1 T. butter

1 onion, chopped

2 small jalapeños, seeded & diced

1 lb. ground beef

1 (1 oz.) pkg. taco seasoning mix

1 (14 oz.) can tomato sauce

1 (14 oz.) can kidney beans, drained & rinsed

1 (14 oz.) can diced tomatoes, drained

8 (1 oz.) bags nacho cheese Doritos

Toppings *(we used fresh tomatoes, jalapeños, radishes & sour cream)*

In a big saucepan over medium heat, melt the butter; add the onion and sauté until just softened. Add the jalapeños and cook 2 to 3 minutes more. Add the ground beef and cook until done, crumbling it while it cooks. Drain, return to the pan, and stir in the taco seasoning.

Dump the tomato sauce, kidney beans, and canned tomatoes into the saucepan with the meat and cook until heated through, stirring occasionally.

Open the bags of Doritos and let everybody build their own taco by scooping some of the meat mixture into the chip bags and adding toppings of their choice. **Makes 8**

PUDDING PACKS 2 GO

*Remove half the wafers from 10 (1 oz.) snack-size bags of Nilla Wafers; set aside. Stand the bags upright in a 9 x 13" pan. Slice 3 or 4 bananas and toss with a little lemon juice. To the wafers in each bag, add a layer of prepared banana pudding and banana slices; repeat layers adding the set-aside wafers. Eat now for crunchy wafers or chill for an hour or two for softer ones. To serve, top with spray whipped cream and a cherry. **Makes 10***

KISS-CAM *Coffee Cake*

1¾ C. sugar, divided

2⅔ C. flour, divided

¾ C. butter *(½ C. cold, ¼ C. softened)*, divided

¾ C. milk

1 (5.3 oz.) container plain Greek yogurt

1 egg

1 T. finely grated lemon zest

3 to 4 T. lemon juice, divided

2½ tsp. baking powder

1½ C. fresh raspberries, plus more for serving

½ C. powdered sugar

Preheat the oven to 350° and grease a 9 x 13" baking pan. Combine 1 cup sugar and ⅔ cup flour; slice the cold butter and cut into the dry ingredients until crumbly; set aside.

In a mixing bowl, beat together the milk, yogurt, egg, lemon zest, 2 tablespoons lemon juice, the remaining ¾ cup sugar, and the softened butter until creamy. In a small bowl, stir together the baking powder and the remaining 2 cups of the flour and beat into the creamy mixture until just blended. Fold in 1½ cups raspberries. Spread the batter into the prepped pan and sprinkle evenly with the set-aside crumb topping. Bake 45 to 50 minutes or until a toothpick inserted comes out with a few crumbs. Set aside until cool.

Mix the powdered sugar with the remaining 1 to 2 tablespoons lemon juice and drizzle over the cooled coffee cake. Serve with more raspberries. **Serves 12**

REVVIN' *Beer Bread*

Preheat the oven to 375° and grease a 5 x 9" loaf pan. In a mixing bowl, combine 3 C. flour, 1 T. baking powder, 1 tsp. salt, and 2 T. sugar; beat in 1 egg until well mixed. Pour in 1 C. of beer *(that cheap pale ale that's hiding in your fridge is just fine)* and mix until the dough becomes sticky and forms a ball; set aside.

In a separate bowl, beat together 8 oz. cream cheese *(softened)*, ½ tsp. onion powder, 1 tsp. garlic salt, ½ to 1 C. diced jalapeños *(fresh or pickled)*, and 1 C. shredded cheddar cheese; fold into the set-aside dough until just mixed. Put the dough into the prepped loaf pan and top with a little more shredded cheddar and some more jalapeño slices. Bake 50 to 60 minutes, until nice and brown. Cool for a bit before removing from the pan. Cool completely before slicing. **Makes 1 loaf**

ALL-STAR *Pickle Wraps*

Mix 2 oz. cream cheese *(softened)* with 3 T. mayo until nice and smooth. Stir in ½ C. finely shredded cheddar cheese, ¼ tsp. garlic powder, and salt and cayenne pepper to taste. Chill for 30 minutes.

Drain 1 (24 oz.) jar Stackers dill pickles and put between layers of paper towels, pressing out as much juice as possible. Spread 1 tsp. of the chilled cream cheese mixture over each pickle slice. Chop 6 thin slices peppered salami and sprinkle evenly over the cream cheese. Roll up and secure with toothpicks. **Makes about 15**

FAN-FAVORITE *Shrimp Packs*

1 (13.5 oz.) pkg. Andouille sausage

3 ears frozen or shucked fresh sweet corn

16 asparagus spears

1 lb. large peeled, cooked shrimp, tails removed

1 (8 oz.) pkg. sliced fresh mushrooms

1 or 2 lemons, sliced

¼ C. olive oil

¼ C. butter, sliced

Salt, black pepper, and Old Bay seasoning to taste

Cut the sausage and corn into chunks and trim the ends off the asparagus spears.

Divide the cut-up food equally among four 18 x 24" sheets of heavy-duty foil that have been spritzed with cooking spray; add equal amounts of shrimp and mushrooms. Lay the lemon slices on top of the food. Drizzle each pack with 1 tablespoon oil; put pats of butter on top and sprinkle with salt, black pepper, and a generous amount of Old Bay. Double fold the tops and ends of the foil, sealing in the food and leaving some room inside for air to circulate.

Grill the packs over medium heat with the lid closed about 15 minutes, until the veggies are crisp-tender and shrimp are opaque, turning the packs once or twice. Open carefully to release steam away from your face. **Serves 4**

BLACK & GOLD BEER

Fill a glass halfway with hard cider, then pour stout beer very slowly over the back of a spoon to fill the glass (we used Angry Orchard and Guinness Draught). If black & gold aren't your team's colors, try other styles and varieties of beer. While certain beers work better than others, keep in mind that practice makes perfect! Happy experimenting!

TOUCHDOWN *Cheese Ball*

- 2 (8 oz.) pkgs. cream cheese, softened
- 1 tsp. Italian seasoning
- 8 oz. finely shredded mozzarella cheese
- ½ C. shredded Parmesan cheese
- 3 green onions, thinly sliced
- ½ C. chopped cooked bacon
- 1 (4 oz.) jar diced pimentos, drained
- 2 (5 oz.) pkgs. mini pepperoni slices, divided
- 1 slice white cheese *(any kind)*
- Crackers, pretzels, and/or breadsticks

Line a small bowl with plastic wrap, letting the ends of the wrap hang over the side of the bowl; set aside.

Beat the cream cheese until light and fluffy. Beat in the Italian seasoning, mozzarella, and Parmesan. Mix in the green onions, bacon, pimentos, and 1 package of the pepperoni. Press the cheese mixture firmly into the bowl and cover with the ends of the plastic wrap. Remove the plastic-covered ball from the bowl and press it into a football shape. Chill at least 2 hours.

Remove the cheese ball from the plastic wrap and let stand 15 minutes. Finish your "football" by covering the cheese ball with more pepperoni slices, pressing to adhere. Cut the slice of cheese into strips and use to decorate the top like football laces. Serve with crackers, pretzels, and/or breadsticks. **Serves a crowd**

ENDZONE